A Crown Of Beauty For Ashes: A Journey Through The Lenten Season

Cycle A Sermons for Lent and Easter
Based on Gospel Texts

Bill Thomas

CSS Publishing Company, Inc.
Lima, Ohio

A CROWN OF BEAUTY FOR ASHES

FIRST EDITION
Copyright © 2022
by CSS Publishing Co., Inc.

Published by CSS Publishing Company, Inc., Lima, Ohio 45807. All rights reserved. No part of this publication may be reproduced in any manner whatsoever without the prior permission of the publisher, except in the case of brief quotations embodied in critical articles and reviews. Inquiries should be addressed to: CSS Publishing Company, Inc., Permissions Department, 5450 N. Dixie Highway, Lima, Ohio 45807.

Library of Congress Cataloging-in-Publication Data:

Names: Thomas, Bill, 1965- author.
Title: A crown of beauty for ashes : a journey through the Lenten season : sermons for Lent and Easter based on the gospel texts / by Bill Thomas.
Description: Lima : CSS Publishing Company, Inc., 2022. | Includes bibliographical references.
Identifiers: LCCN 2022017844 (print) | LCCN 2022017845 (ebook) | ISBN 9780788030581 (paperback) | ISBN 9780788030598 (adobe pdf)
Subjects: LCSH: Bible. Gospels--Sermons. | Lenten sermons. | Easter--Sermons. | Lectionary preaching. | Common lectionary (1992). Year A.
Classification: LCC BS2555.54 .T46 2022 (print) | LCC BS2555.54 (ebook) | DDC 252/.62--dc23/eng/20220608
LC record available at https://lccn.loc.gov/2022017844
LC ebook record available at https://lccn.loc.gov/2022017845

For more information about CSS Publishing Company resources, visit our website at www.csspub.com, email us at csr@csspub.com, or call (800) 241-4056.

e-book:
ISBN-13: 978-0-7880-3059-8
ISBN-10: 0-7880-3059-0

ISBN-13: 978-0-7880-3058-1
ISBN-10: 0-7880-3058-2

Contents

Acknowledgments 5

Ash Wednesday .... Matthew 6:1-6, 16-21
A Crown Of Beauty For Ashes 7

First Sunday in Lent .... Matthew 4:1-11
Tested 11

Second Sunday in Lent .... Matthew 17:1-9
Authentic 15

Third Sunday in Lent .... John 4:5-42
Caring 18

Fourth Sunday in Lent .... John 9:1-41
Seeing 22

Fifth Sunday in Lent .... John 11:1-45
Feeling 25

Passion Sunday .... Matthew 26:14--27:66
Betrayed 29

Maundy Thursday .... John 13:1-17, 31b-35
Serving 33

Good Friday .... John 18:1-19:42
Crucified 36

Resurrection of the Lord/Easter Day .... John 20:1-18
Triumphant 39

Second Sunday of Easter .... John 20:19-31
Life Giver 42

Third Sunday of Easter .... Luke 24:13-35
Unexpected 46

Fourth Sunday of Easter .... John 10:1-10
Gateway 50

Fifth Sunday of Easter .... John 14:1-14
Homebuilder 54

Sixth Sunday of Easter .... John 14:15-21
Presence 57

Ascension of the Lord .... Luke 24:44-53
Ascended 60

Seventh Sunday of Easter .... John 17:1-11
Glorified 64

Acknowledgments

I want to thank David Runk and his team at CSS Publishing for the opportunity to write this book. It has been my joy and honor to work with them for more than a decade. I appreciate their commitment to quality teaching materials for the local church. I am blessed to have a small part in what they do.

I want to thank Dottie Bodewitz at First Christian Church for her help in proofreading and correcting the manuscript. You have always been a great editor and an even better friend.

I want to thank Crystal Applegarth, friend and colleague at Central, for her work in providing her thoughts and careful reading of this manuscript. I appreciate your work and your friendship.

I want to thank Lydia Reeves, friend and student at Central, for her work in proofreading and making sure the final copy is as free from error as it can be. I appreciate your hard work and excellence in that.

Most of all, I want to thank the Lord Jesus Christ. He truly gives beauty for ashes. To him be the glory, now and always.

Ash Wednesday
Matthew 6:1-6, 16-21

A Crown Of Beauty For Ashes

On November 23, 2016, a fire was reported in Great Smoky Mountains National Park near Gatlinburg, Tennessee. The wildfire began burning in a remote location of the park called the Chimney Tops. That area has steep terrain with vertical cliffs and narrow rocky ridges, making access to the wildfire area difficult for firefighters to reach, so quite a bit burned before it could be extinguished. I'd visited the Smoky Mountains numerous times before and was amazed to see the damage this fire did. While most of the park was unaffected by the fire, the parts that were appeared to be a mass of blackened landscape and ash. That part of the countryside lay in ruin.

Though it isn't pleasant to consider, I think most of us know that everything falls apart. Cars break down. Paint chips off. Flowers wilt and turn brittle. Skin wrinkles. Bodies get old and muscles ache. Sometimes, beautiful mountain landscapes burn. Hopes and dreams can turn to ashes, too. Jobs are lost. Children rebel. Marriages grow stale.

I'm convinced that everyone has ashes. Everyone has something in their life that has fallen apart. And now it lies there — our sins, fears, disappointments, and failures — in a heap of ashes.

On this Ash Wednesday, we understand fully that we all need a Savior. We need the effects of Jesus Christ's glorious resurrection to resonate in our lives once more, bringing hope, restoration and a chance for something new. Worship is the key that allows Jesus Christ to minister peace, encouragement, and hope to ashen hearts and lives.

In this text, Jesus challenged his hearers to worship in a genuine, authentic way. He began, "Beware of practicing your piety before others in order to be seen by them; for then you have no reward from your Father in heaven."

Matt Skinner, of Luther Seminary, wrote, "If you act in a way designed to secure the notice of others, your deeds of righteousness yield no reward. Note that this does not disallow public piety. Jesus warned against perverted piety or piety misused for public self-aggrandizement. Those who do this are hypocrites, and they forfeit reward from God."[1]

Acts of worship done for public consumption amount to nothing. As I thought about this, cotton candy came to mind. I know it's a bit unusual but stay with me. Imagine the big, puffy, pink cotton candy that you see at the baseball game or the circus. Cotton candy like that looks awesome, doesn't it? It's like a cloud of pink, sugary deliciousness. As anyone who has had cotton candy knows, though, there is no nutritional value in cotton candy. In fact, there's not much to it at all. It looks great but adds nothing. In fact, too much of it can make you sick. Worship done only for show adds nothing to your spiritual development either.

Jesus addressed three areas that were recognizable acts of piety among Jews and Christians: giving alms, prayer, and fasting. In all three of these areas, he warned against doing them to be noticed by others. Why? Worship for show cannot bring the worshiper nearer to God and does nothing to alleviate the struggle that so many face. Cotton candy can't bring anything up from the ashes.

In these three areas, Jesus advocated for genuine worship. The question wasn't whether his hearers would do these acts. They were expected to do them and likely would give alms, pray, and fast. The issue was how they would do them. Would they give in to the pressure of doing them for show or would their acts of worship be deeper? Would they be genuine?

Genuine worship isn't doing things to be thought of by others as devout or holy. It is the connection of the believer's heart and the heart of God. Genuine worship is what happens at the

---

[1] Matt Skinner, "Ash Wednesday," The Working Preacher, February 25, 2009, https://www.workingpreacher.org/commentaries/revised-common-lectionary/ash-wednesday/commentary-on-matthew-61-6-16-21-5

intersection of divine grace and human frailty. It highlights the glory of Jesus Christ. Simply put, it is keeping our eyes on Jesus Christ.

That sounds simple on the surface, but often isn't. It's easy to let stuff get in the way. We can be overwhelmed by the severity of our struggle. We can be weighed down by the weight of past sins and regret. These things can cause us to no longer see the Lord. Our worship is muted, and the pile of ashes grows larger.

The answer is to see Jesus Christ. Seeing our Lord changes our perspective and outlook. Through worship, the cares and concerns of this temporary world melt away in the splendor of what's eternal. To see Jesus Christ is to see the promise of hope and a fresh start. The first verse and chorus of Helen Howarth Lemmel's song, "The Heavenly Vision," addresses this.

> *O soul are you weary and troubled?*
> *No light in the darkness you see?*
> *There's light for a look at the Savior,*
> *And life more abundant and free!*
> *Turn your eyes upon Jesus,*
> *Look full in his wonderful face,*
> *And the things of earth will grow strangely dim,*
> *In the light of his glory and grace.*[2]
> (in the public domain)

Seeing Jesus Christ not only changes how things look, but can motivate us to acts of worship and service. Throughout these three examples, Jesus makes it clear that God sees what is done in secret and will reward those who worship in that way.

The hours spent in prayer each night, alone in the bedroom, unheard and unnoticed by the world, are noticed and heard by God.

Time spent preparing Sunday school lessons, unseen by the world, are seen by God.

The encouraging word to the troubled youth who lives down the street or cutting the grass of the elderly neighbor never makes

---

2 Helen Howarth Lemmel, "The Heavenly Vision," https://www.godtube.com/popular-hymns/the-heavenly-vision-turn-your-eyes-upon-jesus-/

the nightly news or social media newsfeeds, but it matters to God.

Today, Christians around the world will bear the mark of ashes. It is a somber time of reflection and repentance. Though they are prominent today, these ashes are not the final word in defining who we are. Genuine worship of Jesus Christ reminds us that, in him, we have the promise of new life, hope, and purpose. The passage from Isaiah 61:2-3, which Jesus read a long time ago in the synagogue, rings true today. Of the Messiah's purpose, Isaiah wrote, "to comfort all who mourn, and provide for those who grieve in Zion — to bestow on them a crown of beauty instead of ashes, the oil of joy instead of mourning, and a garment of praise instead of a spirit of despair."

A crown of beauty for ashes — what a wonderful promise.
Amen.

First Sunday in Lent
Matthew 4:1-11

Tested

On January 4, 2018, Polymer Solutions Incorporated released a report titled, "The Top 7 Things We Tested."[3] One of the seven, I found most unusual. They tested NASCAR Stadium seats. The stadium seats had to be tested to make sure they could handle a lot of abuse from fans, multiple cleanings, temperature changes, and consistent exposure to ultra-violet light. That's a lot of tests for a stadium seat! I guess, though, if we want to make sure it's good, it has to be tested.

We begin the Lenten journey on the road of testing, too. However, it's not seats that are being tested. It's Jesus and us.

Every journey has a beginning, and we begin this one by remembering how Jesus Christ started his earthly ministry. Extraordinary events marked his baptism. The Spirit of God descended on him like a dove and a voice from heaven declared, "This is my Son, the beloved, with whom I am well pleased." It is a glorious start. It would be followed by a challenging time of testing and temptation.

Jesus was then led by the Spirit to the wilderness. After forty days of fasting, he's hungry, literally famished. Physically, he's in a weakened condition. The tempter seized this moment to launch his attack. He dangles three temptations to entice Jesus to deviate from the plan the Father laid out for him.

These temptations were real and demonstrate the truth of what the Hebrew writer noted in Hebrews 4:15. "For we do not have a high priest who is unable to sympathize with our weaknesses, but we have one who in every respect has been tested as we are, yet without sin." The Christ who "emptied himself,

---

[3] Polymer Solutions News Team, "Top 7 Things We've Tested," Polymer Solutions Incorporated (January 4, 2018). https://www.polymersolutions.com/blog/interesting-things-tested/

taking the form of a slave, being born in human likeness" (Philippians 2:7) was subject to every human experience. He knew hunger, pain, grief, rejection, and the wide range of human experiences. Had he not, the incarnation would be incomplete. If Jesus could not fail, his temptation was less than our everyday experience.

The words of the first temptation speak to his basic human cravings. "If you are the Son of God, command these stones to become loaves of bread." As he heard these words, we can only imagine how Jesus may have longingly looked to stones that could become bread. Did he consider how great it would feel to satisfy his rumbling stomach?

We know that temptation, too. "Fulfill your wants" is a message we regularly hear. Unbridled and unrestrained attempts to push us to gratify our cravings dominate our media. In many ways, we've been convinced that we deserve everything our hearts desire. Satan, it seemed, hoped Jesus would feel aggrieved. Maybe he would feel that he was owed something. "Satisfy your desires," might have been what Satan whispered to Jesus then and to many of us now.

Jesus rejected that temptation. Quoting from Deuteronomy 8:3, he told the tempter, "It is written, 'One does not live by bread alone, but by every word that comes from the mouth of God.'"

This test is a challenging one. It usually hits us when we are at a weak point, and it promises to provide what we desperately think we want. Jesus' response to this temptation is how we need to respond, too. He refused to consider his physical desires. He looked higher and declared that doing what God had called him to do (God's Word) was more important than the physical cravings of this life. It's a powerful example for us as we begin our Lenten journey.

The tempter isn't finished. The second test is not to satisfy a basic, human need. This one goes deeper. Satan tempted Jesus to make God prove himself. "If you are the Son of God, throw yourself down." He then quotes scripture himself, referencing Psalm 91, which notes that the angels would bear him up.

The temptation to make God prove himself is one that surfaces in our lives, too. Sometimes the tempter plants the thought in our heads, and we can't quite dismiss it. It says, "If God is really God, he'll do this or do that." Occasionally, the temptation is found in the words of others. "If you have enough faith, God will do whatever you need."

Jesus answered the tempter, quoting Deuteronomy 6:16. "Do not put the Lord your God to the test." God is bigger than our contrived tests. Because he sees what we can't, his actions are not easily understood, but they are always right. Jeremy Camp, in an interview about the movie "I Still Believe," echoes this sentiment. Speaking of his and Melissa's story, he said, "I don't understand, but I'll choose to trust you and believe in you."[4]

His first two attempts rebuffed; Satan takes one final shot against Jesus. This temptation is different than the previous two. This one is an attempt to get Jesus to take a shortcut in God's plan. From the time God breathed into Adam's nostrils the breath of life, he knew the day would come that Jesus would have to die for humanity. The plan to become King of kings ran through Golgotha. The tempter, though, offered all the kingdoms of the world without a cross. All Jesus would have to do is bow down and worship Satan. Kingdoms and no cross; that's Satan's offer.

Satan may have hoped that Jesus would accept the idea that the end justified the means. He may have hoped that Jesus would accept the idea that it doesn't matter how you get there as long as you do. That temptation snakes its way into our lives, too. The words sound logical and there seems to be a certain practicality to them. That's misleading, however. It is simply a thin veneer. There's no substance to that kind of thinking. It's an empty, hollow course of action.

There was a right path for Jesus and a wrong one. Shortcuts don't pan out when it comes to the path God has called you to walk. Jesus reiterated that to Satan and told him, "Away with you, Satan! for it is written, 'Worship the Lord your God, and serve only him.'"

---

[4] Matthew Leimkuehler, "'I Still Believe': Inside Jeremy Camp's inspiring (and heartbreaking) big screen story," Nashville Tennessean, March 11, 2020.

At this, Satan left him, and angels came and waited on him. Jesus demonstrated a powerful resolve to trust and obey his father. That's what will sustain him throughout this journey.

Testing and temptation may visit us on our journey, too. When they do, remember what Jesus did. "Trust and obey, there's no other way to be happy in Jesus, but to trust and obey."[5]

---

5   Don Moen, "Trust and Obey," Hymns of Hope (2014).

Second Sunday in Lent
Matthew 17:1-9

Authentic

Whether it is historical documents, antiques, sports memorabilia, or works of art, collectors know that for the item to be valuable it must be authentic. In other words, it has to be the real thing. The Leonardo da Vinci painting "Salvator Mundi" is over six hundred years old and sold for $450 million at an auction in 2017. As recently as 1958, the same painting sold for sixty dollars as skeptics were convinced it was merely a print and not the real thing.[6]

The 1909 Honus Wagner baseball card remains the most valuable baseball card in the world. Even in poor condition, this card will bring in over a million dollars. There are only fifty to 75 genuine Wagner cards in circulation. Because of how much it is worth, Old Sports Cards, a website business dedicated to the hobby of collecting cards, warns against buying fakes.[7]

I read about an authenticated letter from President Abraham Lincoln that, in 2015, sold at auction in Dallas for $2.2 million. It contained the last passage of his second inaugural address, including the famed line, "With malice toward none; with charity for all."[8] That's a rare find and a historical treasure. Why? Because it is the real deal.

The real deal is what matters. As we continue on our Lenten journey, we come to the moment when some of Jesus' disciples find out that he is the real deal. About six days after speaking to

---

6 Aaron Smith, "A $450 million da Vinci is Cool. Here's the Real Reason Rich People Spend Millions on Art," CNN Money (November 17, 2017). https://money.cnn.com/2017/11/16/news/salvator-mundi-leonardo-da-vinci-art/index.html

7 Ross Uitts, "100 Most Valuable Baseball Cards: The All-Time Dream List," Old Sports Cards (August 16, 2021). https://www.oldsportscards.com/most-valuable-baseball-cards/

8 Erik Hoyer, "What Makes Historical Documents Valuable," EJ's Auction & Appraisal (June 16, 2018). https://www.ejsauction.com/makes-historical-documents-valuable/

the disciples in Caesarea Philippi about his identity and telling them that he would die and rise again, Jesus takes Peter, James, and John to a high mountain, Mount Hermon, apart from the others.

What happens while they are on the mountain is incredible. Jesus was transfigured before them. The verb used there is the root word from which we get the English word "metamorphosis." Jesus' face shone like the sun while his clothes became as white as the light. Unlike Moses, whose face radiated God's glory, this glory came from inside Jesus. His identity is on full display. While the curtain is being pulled back on Jesus' identity, Moses and Elijah appear with him and talk to him. It is a remarkable sight.

Peter is struck by what he saw and recognized the significance of it. It may be that he is anticipating the immanent dawn of the Messianic Age. So, he offered, likely in the tradition of the Feast of Tabernacles or Booths where the Jews built shelters for themselves and lived for seven days, to build three shelters, one for each of them. While Peter was not rebuked harshly for his offer, the voice from heaven makes it clear that this is not about the ushering in of the Messianic Age. This was about Jesus. God declared that Jesus is his Son, the one he loves. He demanded that they listen to him.

In this scene, we find Jesus' identity authenticated. Let's take a step back for a moment to gain some perspective on what just happened.

It's interesting that the two times Matthew mentioned a high mountain are the two scenes we've just viewed: Jesus' temptation and Jesus' transfiguration. That's significant because I think we often find ourselves in the valley between these two mountains. On one side is a place of temptation and testing. On the other side is a place of reassurance, hope, and confidence. We have to walk between them sometimes. Life's path takes us to both; a place filled with hopeless desperation, weakness, and fear, where God seems distant and his goodness far removed

— and a place where Jesus' presence seems so authentic, so reassuring, and so satisfying that we're convinced he is all we'll ever need.

Living out our faith is never an easy thing. The apostle Paul compared living out the faith to a race (2 Timothy 4:7). I have a lot of friends who are runners. A long time ago, I ran cross country and I have done a few 5K runs since then. I can honestly say that there has never been a time when running was smooth and easy for me, even when I was in better shape. It was always hard. I do know some people, though, who describe running in those terms. While I can't say I get it, I believe them. There are also times, though, when runners hit the wall. It is really hard and tough to continue. That's the part I know well.

Most of us do, don't we? We are familiar with struggles, difficulties, and disappointments. We wrestle with the death of a loved one, or the somber medical prognosis. We're not strangers to financial difficulties, job struggles, or family squabbles. We know what it means to fail an important exam or to be betrayed by friends.

When those tough times come, be encouraged. Jesus is the real deal. He is the Messiah. I can't help but think of Jesus' cousin, John. He was nearing the end of his ministry and, really, the end of his life. He was in prison, and he was filled with questions. He wanted to know if Jesus really was the one. "Are you the one to come, or should we look for someone else?" (Matthew 11:3). John wanted to know if Jesus was real. Is he authentic? Is he the real deal? Jesus answered John and that answer was reiterated on Mount Hermon.

The hymnwriter Augustus M. Toplady wrote in 1762 these words that still ring true today: "Rock of Ages, cleft for me, let me hide myself in thee. Rock of ages, cleft for me." (in the public domain) That wonderful, old hymn speaks of the reality of Jesus as the Messiah and Savior. We can know and count on him. He's the real thing.

Third Sunday in Lent
John 4:5-42

Caring

Joseph W. Clifton was 37 when he enlisted as a private in the Union army in August 1861. He was much older than most of the men he fought with, yet like many of his comrades, Clifton likely enlisted out of patriotism due to a need for money and merely to escape the doldrums of daily life. At home in the south Jersey town of Burlington, he was the father of five children, and he worked as a stonemason. Serving in the sixth New Jersey Volunteer Infantry, Clifton fought with the Army of the Potomac during the Peninsula Campaign of 1862. As the summer months grew hotter and the combat became more strenuous, Clifton suffered under Virginia's oppressive heat and humidity. Writing from Harrison's Landing, just southeast of Richmond, Clifton described the battles to his brother. But if the fighting was not bad enough, it was horrible to walk through the fields and see only dead soldiers. The experience had a profound impact on the green volunteer. "I never want to see any more fighting for I am sick of it now," he wrote. He wanted to go home to see his family. "I have got another little girl that I never seen yet," he added despondently. Eventually, because of intense pain in his stomach and side, army surgeons sent Clifton to a military hospital in Chester, Pennsylvania. After about four months of recuperation, he decided he'd had enough. On December 5, 1862, Clifton left the hospital without permission. Instead of reporting back to his unit, he went home to Burlington to work and be with his family. Around July 17, 1863, he was arrested and returned to his regiment. Less than a week later he again deserted, this time "while in pursuit of the enemy," as the army was "hourly expecting an engagement." In October, he was captured a second time. Two months later, he was court-martialed and found guilty of desertion. He was sentenced to be shot. The commanding general, George Meade, approved the court's decision and set the execution date for January 29, 1864.

Many people intervened and wrote to President Lincoln about Clifton. Lincoln seemed uncertain of what to do. He'd pardoned many, but pardons were bad for morale, especially pardons for desertion. On April 13, 1865, one day before he was shot and killed by John Wilkes Booth, Abraham Lincoln made his decision. A paper was presented in the military court in Clifton's hometown. There were no words on the paper other than the signature of A Lincoln, the date and the simple word *"Pardoned."*[9]

It was an incredible act of kindness and grace. President Lincoln was a caring man. On our journey through this Lenten season, the caring nature of Jesus is seen, too.

Chapter 4 begins with the Pharisees becoming concerned that Jesus' ministry is growing even larger than John's. Jesus hears of this and decides to travel north to Galilee. Unlike most Jews of his day, though, Jesus decides to go north on the most direct route, through Samaria. Most Jews didn't do that. They made the journey north the long way, going around Samaria. Why? It was simple to them. No self-respecting Jew would have anything to do with Samaritans. The roots of this division were old and deep. The hatred and separation dated all the way back to the days of the patriarchs. The disciples knew it and had lived it.

The fact remains Jesus *had to go* through Samaria. Why? It's possible that he simply had to because of the geographic proximity of Samaria to Galilee, but there's likely more to it. It may well be that a divine appointment had to be kept in the little town of Sychar. It was an opportunity to demonstrate his caring.

As Jesus entered Sychar with his disciples, he was tired from the journey. He sat down by a well in the middle of town while the disciples went to find food. As he was sitting there, a woman approached him. It was about the sixth hour of the day, which

---

[9] Jonathan White, "The Good and Kind Heart of Lincoln," *The New Jersey Monthly*, February 18, 2014.

was an unusual time for a woman to come to the well, but there she was. Maybe she was not welcome at normal hours. Maybe she wasn't wanted in the crowd of other women. Maybe she just needed the water then. We don't know for sure. What we do know is that Jesus spoke to her. She and Jesus had a conversation that covered much more than a drink of water.

Let's pause in the story for a moment to consider what had happened. Jesus was in a place where no good Jew would go. He was having a spiritual conversation with a woman. This was a woman who had had a tough life. A woman in that time and culture was expected to marry and have children. Her security and her worth were often dependent on it. Many people, upon reading this text, believed her to be a woman of questionable morals. It was certainly possible. It may be that she was in a sinful relationship. It was also possible her five husbands died, leaving her a widow. Maybe one or more of the marriages ended in divorce. It could be that she was in a sinful sexual relationship with a man that was not her husband or that the last man she was with was one who had simply taken her in because she had no other place to go. Whatever the case may be, it was obvious that this woman's past had been a painful series of events.

Notice what Jesus didn't do. He didn't act as we might sometimes. He didn't angrily condemn her. He didn't ignore her as if she was no one. He didn't do any of the things that religious people would do. While Satan may have wanted to convince this woman she was worthless, Jesus rejected all of that. Her past may well be one sad thing after another, but Jesus refused to dwell on what was. He reached out to her in love. He talked of what can be. He demonstrated caring, compassion, mercy, and grace.

Looking at what can be. That's an important thing for all of us as we try to follow Jesus. It is far too easy for us to get wrapped up in the past, our own or someone else's. Jesus doesn't see any of us defined by what we once were. Where others see past problems, Jesus sees potential. Where others see a wasted life, Jesus sees a fresh start.

This woman got a chance at new life. Her past would no longer rob her of a future. The town got a revival. Samaritans encountered the Messiah, the one for whom their fathers looked and longed. The disciples got a lesson in racial sensitivity and Jesus, well, I don't know if he ever got a drink, but he certainly gained followers.

On this Lenten journey, remember the compassion and grace of our Lord Jesus. He refuses to keep people in the prison of past sins. He sets the captive free. He did it for a woman of Samaria and he can do it for you, too.

Fourth Sunday in Lent
John 9:1-41

Seeing

Ralph Ellison's novel *The Invisible Man* was published in 1952 and was almost immediately a best-seller and won national book awards. Ellison's book chronicles the story of a young, African American young man and his life's journey. In the prologue to the story, Ellison wrote for his protagonist, "I am invisible, understand, simply because people refuse to see me." It is a powerful line and one that resonates throughout the story.

There are all kinds of "invisible people" in the world. They, like Ellison's character, are invisible because people refuse to see them. One of my favorite names for God is found in Genesis 16 in the story of Hagar and Ishmael fleeing from Sarah. God is called "El Roi" in verse thirteen, which means "the God who sees." There are so many people in our world who are unseen. They are the "invisible people" that often are overlooked, passed, and ignored. Some of these "invisible people" may be around as we journey through Lent on our way to the empty tomb. Will we see them?

Jesus did.

Chapter nine of John's gospel begins with this simple, declarative sentence. "As he went along, he saw a man blind from birth." At the end of the previous chapter, Jesus slipped away from those who wanted to stone him. It was clear he didn't want to be seen by them. Now, though, at the beginning of chapter nine, he saw someone who might not be noticed too often. The disciples, perhaps not actually seeing the man as much as his infirmity, wanted to know why he was in that condition. Whose sin was it? His own sin or his parents? That's what they asked. Jesus looked past that, though, to see the man himself. "He was born blind so that God's works might be revealed in him."

Jesus' next words indicated his purpose. "We must work the works of him who sent me while it is day; night is coming when no one can work. As long as I am in the world, I am the light of the world" (vv. 4-5). The rest of the story? Jesus spat on the ground and made mud. He put it on the man's eyes and told him to wash in the Pool of Siloam. When he did that, he was able to see!

Unfortunately, it seems, he was the only one who could. Those around him remained stuck in blindness, not physical, but spiritual. Neighbors and others who had seen him begging were puzzled and unsure if he was the same guy and just how it was he went around seeing. The man who was formerly blind was brought to the Pharisees. Rather than rejoice that a blind man could see, they wanted to know who and how.

The Jewish religious leaders, though physically able to see, chose to remain blind. They couldn't see Jesus as the Messiah. They couldn't see the man as being anything other than "entirely born in sins" (v. 34). Later, Jesus found this man and asked him if he believed in the Son of Man. The man wanted to know who he was so he could. Jesus told him that he had seen him. He was the one. The former blind man now saw clearly enough to proclaim his belief. Jesus then summarized that encounter. "I came into this world for judgment so that those who do not see may see, and those who do see may become blind."

Those who were used to the blind man and the Jewish religious leaders couldn't see who and what was right before them. Osvaldo Vena wrote, "the man was a social outcast on the assumption that his physical and social conditions were the consequence of his or his parents' sin. He was put in this position by a culture that did not give him enough opportunities to support himself in a dignified manner. But Jesus was about to change all that with a miracle that spoke of the healing power of the marginalized."[10]

---

10 Osvaldo Vena, "Commentary of John 9:1-41," The Working Preacher, March 26, 2017, https://www.workingpreacher.org/commentaries/revised-common-lectionary/fourth-sunday-in-lent/commentary-on-john-91-41-5

Jesus healed the marginalized around him. He saw them and reached out to them in compassion. Will we? The invisible people are all around us.

The single mother who was trying her best to raise her three children was out there. She was trying to get her kids to school and daycare, work a full-time job and provide a home for her family. She was bone tired every night and collapsed into her chair once she had bathed the kids and put them to bed. You might wave to her each morning as she drove by in the old minivan, but do you really see her?

Just off the highway exit where your workplace is there is likely to be a stoplight. Every day a guy with one arm probably stands at that light. He holds a sign, the same one each day. It simply says, "Help please." A few times, when there wasn't a lot of traffic, you've rolled down the window and passed him a few bills. Most of the time, though, you try not to make eye contact and hope the light changes quickly. You know he's there, but do you see him?

The boy is only twelve, but already he's been in trouble with law enforcement. Whenever something's missing in the neighborhood, he's the first suspect. He uses bad language and talks about things no twelve-year-old should. Most of the parents in the neighborhood are reluctant to let their children play with him, and with good reason. He's got a mom and an older brother, but they're not home a lot. He practically raises himself. Most folks in the neighborhood do what they can to avoid him. What about you? Do you see him?

These are the "invisible" people. They are often ignored, unseen, unreached and untouched. The religious leaders of Jesus' day couldn't see people like this. The neighbors and those who were around them could only see what they'd always seen. Jesus' disciples could only see questions about why things were as they were. Only Jesus saw the people. Will we?

Fifth Sunday in Lent
John 11:1-45

Feeling

Remember when you were so tired that all you wanted to do was fall into bed, but your baby wouldn't go to sleep when you tried to lay her down? Remember when you intended to work in your garden only to be interrupted by a neighbor who needed something? Remember when you planned a Saturday bike ride along the river trail and had to cancel it because a family member needed help moving a washer and dryer? Sometimes things don't work out like we hope they will. In the small things of life, it is an annoyance.

There are times, though, when the big things don't work out. Perhaps you planned to have your grandparents at your wedding, but your grandfather passed three months before the ceremony. Maybe you hoped to take your parents on a trip back east, but they became too ill before you could make it happen. Maybe you were hoping for the job promotion that went to the guy in the next cubicle. What's an irritation in the small things can be devastating in the big things. Having someone with you who knows what that's like is important. When we're feeling it, we want to know that someone out there knows how we feel.

Jesus knows how you feel. He gets it. He became human, one of us, to walk where we walk. The Hebrew writer noted, "For we do not have a high priest who is unable to sympathize with our weaknesses, but we have one who in every respect has been tested as we are, yet without sin." Jesus understands what it means to be a human being. He understands temptation. He knows rejection, betrayal, weariness, and sorrow. If anyone knows how you feel in those low moments, it's Jesus.

Of all the tough times we go through, perhaps the most difficult is wrestling with the loss of a loved one. Death is a daunting specter for lots of people. According to the 2017 "Survey of American Fears" conducted by Chapman University, 20.3% of Americans are "afraid" or "very afraid" of dying.[11] I think we understand that, don't we? Death can seem so harsh and sad. When a friend or family member dies, it can really hurt.

The summer after my senior year of high school I had the opportunity to work for one of our local funeral homes. I know that sounds unusual for a summer job just out of high school, but it was pretty good money and a great learning experience. While there I saw nearly fifty funerals and how people interacted and dealt with grief and loss. I also washed and waxed a lot of cars and cut grass. Funerals tend to make people uneasy, and I get that. There is a sense of sadness and loss. We sometimes struggle using the word itself. We tend to soften it by saying things like, "they've passed on," "they passed away," or "they went to be with the Lord." The words *death* and *died* are scary. They appear so permanent; so final.

On this Lenten journey, we see Jesus remind those in Bethany and us today that he is greater than death. His encounter with Martha and Mary at the death of Lazarus shows us the depth of his feeling.

Lazarus died and his sisters, Mary and Martha, stood at the intersection of disappointment and despair. Four days earlier they sent a message to Jesus. His friend, Lazarus, was sick and dying. They pleaded with Jesus to come and expected him to do so. He didn't, though. Lazarus died and the sisters were left in pools of grief and questions of "what if." A broken heart can hurt all over.

Jesus understood the pain of a broken heart. His words to Martha and Mary, and his tears at finding out where Lazarus was buried, indicated the depth of his feelings. He was powerful and direct in his declaration that the grave was not the final destination, and for those who know and love Jesus Christ, death

---

11 Angela Morrow, "When Your Fears About Dying Are Unhealthy," VeryWell Mind (November 28, 2019). https://www.verywellmind.com/scared-to-death-of-death-1132501

need not be feared. Jesus felt the heartache of both Martha and Mary. He reminded them and us that he is the resurrection and the life. The ones who believe in him will never die.

John 11:35 is a verse that children throughout church history have memorized as one of the shortest in the English New Testament. It reveals an important truth. "Jesus began to weep." These are simple words that speak a profound spiritual truth. What is the occasion for these words? When Jesus saw Mary weeping and the Jews with her weeping, he was "deeply moved in spirit and troubled." He felt their grief and loss. He was emotionally touched, and he wept.

Why did Jesus weep? He didn't weep because Lazarus was dead. He knew what he was about to do. I don't think he wept because people he loved were trapped in the grip of despair. He was about to demonstrate how fragile that hold really was.

His weeping, I think, had a lot to do with the fact that Jesus knew, understood, and cared about the pain that his friends felt and were going through. What hurt them hurt him. I think he also wept because the stench of Satan soils the lives of those he loves. He was about to reverse this death, but even for a moment, seeing the fingerprints of Satan on the lives of those he loved broke his heart and brought him to tears. He wept because people mattered to him and when they were sad, it touched him deeply. The simple truth that Jesus wept brings comfort, encouragement, and hope. When we weep, we do not weep alone. This account shows us, in unmistakable honesty, how much Jesus feels our pain and knows our sorrow. Jesus knows what you're facing and what you're going through.

He feels our anxiety when the stack of bills is higher than the monthly income.

He feels our uncertainty when the problem seems to have no good answer.

He feels the stabbing pain we do when we hear the words "I don't love you anymore."

He feels our hurt when our kids follow the path of the prodigal.

He feels our concern when the doctors say there's nothing more that they can do.

He feels our grief at the grave of a loved one gone too soon.

This Lenten journey shows us a lot about Jesus. On his way to the cross and his own tomb, Jesus stopped at the tomb of his friend Lazarus. He felt the sorrow and reminded those there that death is temporary and not to be feared. Understand that Jesus feels what we do. He gets it.

Passion Sunday
Matthew 26:14--27:66

Betrayed

Les Parrott wrote, "Backstabbers specialize in saying the wrong thing at the wrong time to the wrong person."[12] Backstabbing and betrayed are not words that we want or like to hear. Unfortunately, most of us are painfully aware of the betrayer's sting.

A friend promised to be there for you but you haven't seen him in months.

She told you she would be yours forever but now she's with someone else, maybe saying the same thing.

He'd promised to keep your secret but he didn't. It's out and everyone knows.

She said she'd come. She promised. But she didn't and you're left by yourself, again.

Betrayal is not a new thing. In August 480 BC, during the second Persian invasion of Greece, a small Greek force under the Spartan king Leonidas defended Greece against the southward advance of Xerxes' Persian army. Leonidas's troops held the pass at Thermopylae for three days. It was a stalemate until they were betrayed. The Persians, guided along another mountain pass by the Greek Ephialtes, outflanked them. Sending the majority of his troops to safety, Leonidas remained to delay the Persians with 300 Spartans, all of whom died in battle. Although the Persians won at Thermopylae and conquered central Greece, they suffered considerable losses in the battle. This battle became celebrated in history and literature as an example of heroic

---

12 Les Parrott, *High Maintenance Relationships: How to Handle Impossible People* (Wheaton, Illinois: Tyndale House Publishers, 1996), 103.

resistance against great odds. Ephialtes became known as the "Greek traitor."[13]

Traitors, betrayers, backstabbers; history is littered with their names. Ephialtes, Benedict Arnold, Vidkung Quisling, and Marcus Junius Brutus are among them. These traitors are infamous for their duplicitous actions. Perhaps the most well-known, though, is Judas Iscariot. During this Lenten season, we visit a tough moment in Jesus' walk. He's betrayed by one of his chosen twelve. How does he respond? What does he do? It's an account that speaks to us in real ways, too, as we continue our journey.

The scene was the last supper. After washing the disciples' feet, Jesus was eating with them. Judas Iscariot had already made a pact with the Jewish religious leaders. He had already agreed to betray Jesus for thirty pieces of silver. This night was his opportunity. The time had come. Jesus was aware of what was happening. He announced with chilling words, "one of you will betray me." The disciples looked to one another in shock and disbelief. Jesus, though, made it clear who it was…the *one who had dipped his hand into the bowl with me.*

Though we don't read what the disciples thought about Jesus' words, we know what happened. Judas Iscariot left the group to embark on the road of betrayal. In a matter of hours, he would deliver the betrayer's kiss and Jesus will be led away. Judas' story was a sad one. We know that once he realized what was going on, he was filled with regret. Desperate to do something, he threw the money back at the religious leaders. In harsh bluntness, Matthew 27:5 noted his end; "he went and hanged himself."

This story is told often, but usually from how Judas is viewed. What about Jesus? Because he was fully God, Jesus knew what was going on with Judas and what he'd done. He wasn't surprised as we sometimes are, but I'm not sure that mitigated the sorrow or pain he must've felt. Jesus possibly felt a twinge of disappointment as he saw Judas coming with a band of soldiers. The betrayer's kiss, no doubt, stung on his cheek. He'd

---

13 Richard Pallardy, "Thermopylae," Encyclopedia Britannica. https://www.britannica.com/place/Thermopylae#ref242315

just washed Judas' feet as an act of love and service, and now, he comes to sell him out.

We might know a bit about betrayals, too. When it happens, there can be, at first, a sense of surprise. Thoughts race through our minds. *How could he do that? I never thought she'd say that. Why? What is he doing?* Betrayal is not normally done by someone we don't know. "The saddest thing about betrayal is that it never comes from your enemies."[14] Betrayal comes from those we know, or at least thought we knew. That's what makes the sting even more painful and the hurt more deep.

After the sense of surprise dissipates, a sense of anger can move in. This is when thoughts of revenge and payback build up in our minds. It's a natural, human impulse to want to strike back, get even, or make the other person pay. We've heard the expression, "Revenge is a dish best served cold." This expression comes from the French around 1800 and means that revenge is more satisfying when one has had time to prepare vengeance that is well-planned, long feared, or unexpected.[15] We know, though, that this is not God's way. Romans 12:19-21 reminds us of that.

Beloved, never avenge yourselves, but leave room for the wrath of God; for it is written, "Vengeance is mine, I will repay, says the Lord." No, "if your enemies are hungry, feed them; if they are thirsty, give them something to drink; for by doing this you will heap burning coals on their heads." Do not be overcome by evil, but overcome evil with good.

Paul made it clear how God wants us to deal with those who wound us with betrayal. We are not to respond in kind, but kindly. That's not hard to read or write, but incredibly hard to do. It can be devastating to see someone we know and care about do something so destructive and harmful.

I often wonder what Jesus was thinking and what the look on his face was as Judas drew near to kiss him. We don't know.

---

14 Anonymous quote, https://www.goodreads.com/quotes/7196306-the-saddest-thing-about-betrayal-is-that-it-never-comes

15 "What does 'Revenge is a Dish Best Served Cold' Mean?," *Writing Explained* (Accessed July 14, 2021). https://writingexplained.org/idiom-dictionary/revenge-is-a-dish-best-served-cold

What we do know is what he said. "Friend, do what you are here to do." Did you catch that? Jesus called him, "Friend." On the road to the cross, Jesus looked into the face of his betrayer, not with anger, rage, or hate. He called him, "Friend."

Somewhere on our journey, we will face betrayal. When we do, turn to Jesus. He's been down that road.

Maundy Thursday
John 13:1-17, 31b-35

Serving

"I expect to pass through this world but once; any good thing therefore that I can do, or any kindness that I can show to any fellow-creature, let me do it now; let me not defer or neglect it, for I shall not pass this way again."[16] This quote is attributed to various people, including Henry Drummond, William Penn, and Stephen Grellet. I'm not sure it matters much who said it. What is important is the meaning of the words themselves. Serving and performing acts of kindness make a big difference. As we draw near to Jesus' death on this Lenten journey, let's pause for a moment in the upper room to catch a glimpse of love and a servant's heart.

It was Thursday. Jesus and his disciples were gathered together. During the supper, Jesus did something extraordinary. He got up from the table, wrapped a towel around his waist, poured water in a basin and began to wash the disciples' feet. That's not what the rabbi ought to do. A servant should have done it, and any of the disciples could have. Many times, if a person was wealthy enough to have slaves, the slave would do it for the guests. In this case, though, no one did. So, Jesus did it.

Craig R. Koester wrote, "For a free person to wash someone else's feet meant that he or she was assuming the position of a slave. The only reason someone would do this voluntarily was to show complete devotion to another person."[17]

Complete devotion: that's the mindset of a servant and it's the heart of Jesus. He loved his disciples and wanted to demonstrate that love as he neared the end of his earthly ministry. We

---

16 "I Expect to Pass Through This World But Once," English Club (Accessed July 15, 2021). https://www.englishclub.com/listening/poetry-pass.htm

17 Craig Koester, "Commentary on John 13:1-17, 31b-35," Working Preacher, April 1, 2010, https://www.workingpreacher.org/commentaries/revised-common-lectionary/maundy-thursday/commentary-on-john-131-17-31b-35-2

can only imagine the scene. The disciples stared awkwardly at each other as Jesus knelt at their feet. He went from John to perhaps James. Maybe Judas Iscariot was next. Then he came to Peter. Peter protested, but Jesus quieted that objection, noting that unless one was washed, he could have no part in him. There was a hint of foreshadowing, though, as Jesus announced that not all of them were clean.

Jesus, before he entered the most difficult and challenging part of his journey, took time to give his disciples a message. The message was clear, simple, and direct. "I love you." Is there any more important message that the disciples could have received than that? In a short time, they would be facing one of the most confusing and agonizing times of their lives. I wonder, did they ever glance at their feet and remember the time their master washed them? Did they remember when he showed them the full extent of his love?

This message resonates with us, too. Often our journey is marked with confusing, tough times that leave us wondering whether the Lord is still with us. When those times come, remember when Jesus, the Lord of all, stooped to wash feet. Think of his great love, the love he had for his disciples then and now. May you never forget the words you learned as a child, "Jesus loves me, this I know."[18]

Having been immersed in his love, Jesus gave them a challenge; wash one another's feet. Jesus was urging them to serve as he served. That challenge echoes through the corridors of time. Jesus revealed something radical. "I give you a new commandment, that you love one another. Just as I have loved you, you also should love one another. By this everyone will know that you are my disciples, if you have love for one another" (vv. 34-35).

Love one another. The word here is the one for unconditional love. It doesn't matter if love is returned, we are to love anyway. How is that love shown? By serving and doing for one another. All around us, there are so many opportunities to love and serve. Let's fill the basin and get a towel.

[18] Anna Bartlett Warner, "Jesus Loves Me," *Hymnary* (1859). https://hymnary.org/text/jesus_loves_me_this_i_know_for_the_bible

Volunteering to watch or take to school the three kids of the single mom who lives down the street is a way to wash her feet.

Spending an hour each week talking to a lonely widower is a way to wash his feet.

You wash the feet of a neighbor when you shovel their driveway, cut their grass, or take their trash out to the curb.

An email, text, or letter in the mail to someone who is lonely and in need of a friend is a way to wash their feet.

All of these have a common denominator. They are acts of service and sacrifice motivated by love. Tara Stackpole knew a little bit about love, service, and giving your all. She wrote this about her husband, Timothy:

> *On June 5, 1998, firefighter Timothy Stackpole was severely injured in a five-alarm fire in Brooklyn. Two of his fellow firefighters were killed and more injured in a collapse. Timmy spent over two months in the burn center with fourth and fifth degree burns over 40% of his body. He endured many surgeries and months of painful rehabilitation. He had two goals: to recover and spend as much time as he could with his family, and to return full-duty to a job he loved. Against popular opinion, he succeeded. On March 10, 2001, Timmy returned to his lieutenant's job full-duty. He was promoted to Captain on September 6, 2001, and was in FDNY headquarters, off-duty, the morning of September 11. Of course, he responded.*
>
> *Timmy had a huge heart, and shared his faith, compassion, and love with everyone he met. His remarkable story has inspired many and his love for the job has touched many firefighters across the country.*[19]

Serving when motivated by love makes a huge difference. This stop on the Lenten journey touches us deeply and in profound ways. We drink deeply of the love Jesus has for us and then we recognize the challenge he's set before us. Serving and love; Jesus demonstrated that on the night of his arrest. Will we follow his example?

---

19 Tara Stackpole, "Roll of Honor: Timothy M. Stackpole," National Fallen Firefighters Foundation (June 5, 1998). Accessed July 16, 2021. https://www.firehero.org/fallen-firefighter/timothy-m-stackpole/

Good Friday
John 18:1-19:42

Crucified

This Lenten journey takes us to an awkward and painful stop. Geographically, it's just outside the city of Jerusalem at a place known as the "Place of the Skull." It's tempting to rush past this ugly place. After all, what took place here was brutal, agonizing, and hard to watch. Who would want to linger here and think about the beaten and battered body of Jesus? Who would want to picture the iron spikes that pierced his hands and feet? Who wants to hear the agonized echo of his cry, "It is finished"? It's not that we are ungrateful for what Jesus did, it's just that it's a painful sight. The road on this journey, though, must pass Golgotha. Crucified is a critical part of what happened.

Sacrifice has always been the reason Jesus came. Paul wrote in 1 Timothy 1:15, "The saying is sure and worthy of full acceptance, that Christ Jesus came into the world to save sinners." There's something profoundly moving about one giving their life for another. Brad Walden shared this story.

The mother of a nine-year-old boy named Mark received a phone call in the middle of the afternoon. It was the teacher from her son's school.

"Mrs. Smith, something unusual happened today in your son's third grade class. Your son did something that surprised me so much that I thought you should know about it immediately."

Mark's mom began to worry.

The teacher continued, "Nothing like this has happened in all my years of teaching. This morning I was teaching a lesson on creative writing. And as I always do, I tell the story of the ant and the grasshopper: The ant works hard all summer and stores up plenty of food. But the grasshopper plays all summer and doesn't work. Then winter comes. The grasshopper begins to starve because he has no food. So, he begins to beg, 'Please Mr. Ant, you have much food. Please let me eat, too.' Then I said, "Boys and girls, your job is to write the ending to the story. Your son, Mark, raised his hand. 'Teacher, may I draw a picture?' Well, yes, Mark, if you like, you may draw a picture. But first you must write the ending to the story.' As in all the years past, most of the students said the ant shared his food through the winter, and both the ant and the grasshopper lived. A few children wrote, 'No, Mr. Grasshopper. You should have worked in the summer. Now, I have just enough food for myself.' Hence, the ant lived, and the grasshopper died. But your son ended the story in a way different from any other child, ever. He wrote, 'So the ant gave all of his food to the grasshopper; the grasshopper lived through the winter. But the ant died.' And the picture he drew? At the bottom of the page, Mark had drawn three crosses."[20]

Three crosses. That picture resonates in our minds, especially today. Something important happened on this day a long time ago. Something we should never forget. To understand what Jesus did on the cross just outside of Jerusalem is to understand, at least at a basic level, what grace is. For something to be given for nothing, a price had to be paid. Mark understood that. In order for the grasshopper to live the ant had to make a sacrifice. In order for fallen man to live, Jesus had to be crucified.

What does the cross mean to us today?

Philip Yancey wrote in his book *Where Is God When It Hurts?*, "Love was compressed for all history in that lonely figure on the cross, who said that he could call down angels at any moment on a rescue mission but chose not to — because of us. At Calvary, God accepted his own unbreakable terms of justice."[21]

The cross represents God's justice. We get that. What Paul wrote in Romans 3:23 is true; "all have sinned and fallen short of the glory of God." God cannot change or compromise who he

---

20 Brad Walden, "Grasshoppers and Ants," December 3, 2011, https://www.realtimefaith.net/assets/earliteens/StudySheets/2011/4Q/Q4YB--Lesson%2010%20Identity%20(4)%20Focused.pdf

21 Philip Yancey, *Where is God When It Hurts?*, Zondervan, Grand Rapids, MI, 1990, p. 205.

is. Because he is holy and just, there has to be a cost for sin. The cross represents that cost.

Though I think it may be hard at times to grasp, we know that the cross should have been ours. There was a time when the imposing shadow of the cross loomed large in our lives, reminding us of our sin, failure and hopelessness. The cross stood as an ugly reminder of death and defeat.

Because of Jesus, however, death has been swallowed up in victory. The cross no longer stands for defeat. Jesus won the battle against sin and death on that cross. The innocent died so the guilty might live. Today, we can wear the cross as an emblem of hope and new life. The cross symbolizes how the debt of sin has been paid. Jesus cried out, "It is finished" (v. 30). The word is *tetelestai* and was often written on business documents or receipts in New Testament times to show indicating that a bill had been paid in full.[22]

What drove and held Jesus to the cross? It wasn't the Roman soldiers, though they were imposing. It wasn't the Jewish officials, though they did not object. It wasn't the iron spikes, though they were horrible. What drove and held Jesus to the cross was love. Jesus loved people, you and me, so much that he willingly went to the cross. He chose to die. His life wasn't taken from him. He gave it away.

As we stop just outside of Jerusalem on this Lenten journey, let's reflect a moment on the cross of Jesus. As odd as it sounds, the cross is the exclamation of Jesus' love.

---

[22] "What does the Greek word 'Tetelestai' Mean?," *Bible.org* (January 1, 2001). https://bible.org/question/what-does-greek-word-tetelestai-mean

Resurrection of the Lord/Easter Day
John 20:1-18

Triumphant

I'm a fan of the Peanuts cartoon strip. I think Charles Schultz did a marvelous job tapping into the human experience with the kids he drew over the years. There's one that especially stands out to me because I think it cuts deeply to what it's like to experience disappointment. I'll describe the strip for you. Imagine Charlie Brown sitting on a bench at school. His lunch bag is next to him. In the first panel he says, "There's that little red-haired girl. She's handing out valentines." The next panel shows an excited, eager Charlie Brown as he says, "She's handing them out to all her friends ... She's handing them out one by one ... She's handing them out ... She's still handing them out ..." The third panel shows Charlie Brown sitting back, his shoulders slumped. He says, "Now she's all done ... That was the last one ... Now she's walking away...." The fourth panel poignantly shows Charlie Brown, his mouth now a quivering upside-down arc, his eyes wide, wobbly, and slightly askew. He looks as if he is trying desperately not to cry. His final word balloon is a simple, ironic "Happy Valentine's Day!"[23]

If there ever was a cartoon that captured discouragement and disappointment, it's that one. I like it, though, because I think Schultz has captured something real. It's a feeling we all know. As we continue on this Lenten journey, we come to an important place just outside the city. It is a tomb. It seems like it ought to be a place of sadness, disappointment and grief. Certainly, that was the feeling that bore down on the followers of Jesus after his death. Many of his disciples deserted him and ran for their lives. They hid, fearing they could be arrested next. Peter denied

---

[23] Bruce Handy, "The Paradox of Peanuts," The Atlantic, August 29, 2019, https://www.theatlantic.com/entertainment/archive/2019/08/charlie-brown-charles-schulz-peanuts-papers-excerpt/596878/

him. Judas Iscariot, his betrayer, took his own life. Uncertainty and dread came with daybreak. For the followers of Jesus, the 48 hours that began early Friday morning were marked by chaos, fear, and confusion. Now, as the first day of the week dawned, dreams were dead, and hope laid lifeless behind a huge stone.

Fear, chaos, and confusion; we understand these words. Our lives are frequently visited by this troubling triplet. They show up the first morning after she's taken the kids and told you she doesn't love you anymore. They stand next to you in the doctor's office as the words "nothing more we can do" reverberate in your heart and mind. They intrude upon your quiet, reflective moment at the gravesite of a loved one gone much too soon. They mock and ridicule as you get the word that your job is gone. You've been downsized. They like to cozy up at the bar and urge you to drink away your sorrows, numb yourself to reality, and try to pretend it doesn't matter.

Fear, chaos, and confusion may have walked with Mary Magdalene on the morning of the first day of the week. The sabbath has come and gone. As we see in the other gospel accounts, Mary Magdalene and some women have come to the tomb to finish the burial. The beginning of the sabbath brought about a rushed sense of getting the body off the cross and into the tomb, so Mary and the others came on the first day of the week to perform one final act of kindness. There's nothing left to do but finish it out. Every step taken on this lonesome road is hard, but necessary.

In the suffocating darkness, a surprising light shined causing fear, chaos, and confusion to tremble. When the women arrived at the tomb, they noticed a remarkable thing. The stone was rolled away. There was no body in the tomb. We learn from Matthew and Luke that the other women encountered the angels and then ran back to the eleven. Mary Magdalene, though, immediately ran to Peter and John and told them of her discovery, "They have taken away my Lord, and I do not know where they have laid him." Peter and John ran to see if what Mary told them was really true. It couldn't be, could it? Peter and John raced to see as Mary followed.

Both Peter and John viewed the empty tomb and returned to where they were staying. Mary, though, encountered two angels in the tomb where the body of Jesus had been. After answering their question, she turned to see a man she doesn't recognize. He asked her why she'd been crying and who she was looking for. She thought he was a gardener, and told him about Jesus and pleaded, "Sir, if you have carried him away, tell me where you have laid him, and I will take him away."

Then, the man uttered a one-word reply, a name, actually. He said, "Mary." Maybe it was the way he said it. Maybe at that moment the veil of darkness was lifted. Maybe the shadow gave way to the light. Whatever the cause, it was at that moment that Mary realized that this man was no gardener. He was her Lord. Jesus was alive. She was overcome and fell at his feet. Jesus told her not to hold on to him, but to go and tell his brothers that he had risen. Jesus is alive!

Can there be any greater news than that to one who is mired in the darkness of defeat? Jesus is alive. Death was disarmed as Jesus triumphed over the grave. Victory devoured fear. Chaos was swallowed up in peace. Confusion cowered in the presence of confidence. This is the message of Easter. This is the shout that reverberates from the empty tomb.

Paul wrote in 1 Corinthians 15:54-57, "When this perishable body puts on imperishability, and this mortal body puts on immortality, then the saying that is written will be fulfilled: "Death has been swallowed up in victory." "Where, O death, is your victory? Where, O death, is your sting?" The sting of death is sin, and the power of sin is the law. But thanks be to God, who gives us the victory through our Lord Jesus Christ."

I read of an inscription found on a small new gravestone after a devastating air raid on Britain in World War II. It simply says, "There is not enough darkness in all the world to put out the light of one small candle." At the midpoint of our journey, we reach an incredibly significant site. It's a tomb with no body. Jesus isn't there. He's risen. He's the light that can't be snuffed out by the darkness. He triumphed over the grave so that all who know him can have that same victory.

Second Sunday of Easter
John 20:19-31

Life Giver

You probably haven't heard of a young man named Kyle McMahan, and that's unfortunate because he has a remarkable story. It was an ordinary night in December when then sixteen-year-old McMahan was driving and noticed headlights at the bottom of a ravine. Instead of continuing to drive by, he decided to stop and take a look. He couldn't believe what he found. WPSD of Union County, Illinois reports what McMahan said. "I got over there. I saw his body, just lying there with his head stuck in the door." The man's head was pinned by the driver's side door and was blocked by a tree. "I could see him with his head stuck in there. I could hear him screaming for help." So, McMahan called the police and stayed with the man until they arrived. For that, he was awarded the Lifesaving Award from the Union County Sherriff's Department.[24]

There's something heroic and heartwarming about those who rescue and save the lives of others. As Frederick Buechner once said, "The world needs people who save lives."[25] We are now moving through the thrilling part of our Lenten journey. As we do, we get to experience the greatest rescue story ever. Like the apostles after the resurrection, we get to see Jesus, the one who gives life.

In the concluding verses of John 20, we see John's purpose for writing. "Now Jesus did many other signs in the presence of his disciples, which are not written in this book. But these are written so that you may come to believe that Jesus is the Messiah,

---

[24] Logan Gay, "Local Teen Recognized for Saving Man's Life," WPSD Local News (January 17, 2018). https://www.wpsdlocal6.com/news/local-teen-recognized-for-saving-man-s-life/article_ec13ad26-1aa3-5469-a3d0-b92558d3f39b.html WPSD Local 6, January 17, 2018.

[25] Frederick Buechner, "Frederick Buechner Extended Interview," *Religion & Ethics Newsweekly* (May 5, 2006). https://www.pbs.org/wnet/religionandethics/2006/05/05/may-5-2006-frederick-buechner-extended-interview/15358/

the Son of God, and that through believing you may have life in his name." Did you catch the last part? "That through believing, you may have life in his name." Jesus did what he did, so that if one accepts him, they can have life. What an incredible gift!

Life is valuable, precious, and sometimes taken for granted. What if you were challenged to summarize your life in six words? What would you write? Inspired by the legendary challenge posed to Ernest Hemingway to write a six-word story that resulted in the classic "For sale: baby shoes, never worn," Smith Magazine asked that question of its readers. The magazine was flooded with so many responses that the site almost crashed. The responses were turned into a book by Rachel Fershleiser and Larry Smith called *Not Quite What I Was Planning*. This book is filled with six-word memoirs by many different writers. The entries range from funny to ironic to inspiring to heartbreaking: "One tooth, one cavity; life's cruel." "Savior complex makes for many disappointments." "Cursed with cancer. Blessed with friends." (This one was written not by a wise, old grandmother but by a nine-year-old boy with thyroid cancer.) "The psychic said I'd be richer." "Thought I would have more impact."[26]

I thought about this challenge in connection with Jesus' post-resurrection appearances to his disciples. They had run the emotional gamut, and now, to see Jesus, they had to know life would never be the same. I wondered what they might have written if they were to capture their thoughts in just six words.

For those unsure of the future, they may have written, "Jesus is alive. What comes next?"

Knowing they'd abandoned him, some may have written, "He's here. Am I in trouble?"

Perhaps those with theological insight would have written, "He lives so I can, too."

Until Jesus' second appearance, Thomas may have penned the words, "I can't believe until I see."

What would you write? Jesus offers life, hope, healing, and heaven to those who believe. Recognizing this and knowing

---

[26] Smith Magazine, *Not Quite What I Was Planning: Six Word Memoirs by Writers Famous and Obscure*, ed. Rachel Fershleiser and Larry Smith (New York: Harper Perennial, 2008).

your own life's journey, what would your six-word life summation be?

Jesus' initial appearance to his disciples brought them three things: peace, power, and purpose. He offered them peace. The word used here implies "peace with God." Since the encounter with Satan in Eden, humans have struggled with sin which separated the Creator from his creation. On this day, Jesus declared that struggle is over. Sin and its partner, guilt, no longer have any sway or power over the one who believes in Jesus.

Jesus pointed to the source of the apostles' power when he breathed on them and said, "Receive the Holy Spirit." Though the indwelling of the Holy Spirit will happen later in the book of Acts, this passage may evoke the original creation of humanity (when God breathed into Adam the breath of life) and indicated that Jesus would keep his promise to send the Holy Spirit to equip and empower them.

He also touched on their purpose. They would represent him and the Father as they interacted with people. He spoke of forgiving sins. While only the Lord can forgive sins, Jesus empowered the apostles, through the work of the Holy Spirit, to distinguish genuine repentance in a person and to acknowledge when it is there and call it out when it is not. We see this occur several times throughout the book of Acts.

Peace, power, and purpose: Jesus offers that to us today, too. In this journey through life, have you been weighed down by the weight of regret, guilt, and sin? Has your work for the Lord been hindered by Satan's nagging reminders of what you once were? The one who gives life offers you peace. Because of his sacrifice, that which separated you from God is no more. What Jesus did a long time ago means your past does not have to impact your present and your future.

Have you ever tried to create lasting change in your life only to find yourself doing the same bad things over again? By our own power, we are not able to change. Jesus offers transformation through the gift of the indwelling Holy Spirit. Yielding to the direction of the Holy Spirit can bring needed change and hope to your life.

That leads to our purpose. Have you ever wondered what you are supposed to do as a follower of Jesus? The one who gives life makes it clear. Represent. We are to represent Jesus in all we do and wherever we go.

Peace, power and purpose; that's a trio with whom I'd travel anytime. Seeing Jesus as the disciples did is refreshing and challenging. What is my life about? Six words? Here's my thought.

May Jesus find me faithful — always.

Third Sunday of Easter
Luke 24:13-35

Unexpected

"I didn't see that coming." We hear that a lot when people encounter the unexpected. Sometimes, it's a dejected summation of a bad situation. You hear a *THUD* of a flat tire as you drive down the highway. As you wrestle the jack out of the trunk, it's possible you might utter, "I didn't see that coming."

You might think you are meeting your spouse for a quiet dinner only to find the whole restaurant full of friends for your surprise party. "Didn't see that coming" could be your pleased response.

Your favorite team shocks the world and wins the championship game. A thrilled "I didn't see that coming" might just be your exclamation. The unexpected often leaves us at a loss and surprised.

On the road to Emmaus, two disciples of Jesus had an unexpected encounter that might have left them stammering, "I didn't see that coming." This account is only found in Luke's gospel and begins abruptly with the words "now on that same day two of them… ." The day noted here was the day Jesus rose from the dead. Who are those disciples on the road to Emmaus? There is no clear antecedent in the first part of chapter 24. They are clearly not part of the eleven within the original circle of the twelve, since the story ends with them going to report to the eleven what had happened (24:33). They are part of a group of disciples to which the women who had gone to the tomb also belong. We are given the name of one of the two on the road to Emmaus, Cleopas, but he isn't mentioned any other time in the New Testament.

These two obscure followers of Jesus had no idea who Jesus was when he approached them. They were aware, however, of recent events in Jerusalem and were incredulous when he asked them about what they were discussing. They shared with Jesus a brief history of all that he did and how he was a prophet, mighty in deed and word before God and all the people. They were quite familiar with the last few days. "Our chief priests and leaders handed him over to be condemned to death and crucified him," they dejectedly reported. They followed that with words that expressed the deep disappointment of their hearts. "But we had hoped that he was the one to redeem Israel."

"But we had hoped..." These words reveal broken dreams and shattered expectations. We're all too familiar with these words, aren't we?

– But we had hoped the cancer would stay in remission.
– But we had hoped the marriage would last.
– But we had hoped the promotion would come.
– But we had hoped the money would last.
– But we had hoped to have children by now.

For Cleopas and his companion, the sorrow and pain of the previous day's events shrouded their eyes and clouded their vision. They were blinded to the amazing reality that walked right beside them. All their sorrowful hearts can put forth is, "but we had hoped."

Disappointment is not a stranger to most of us. Certainly, it was not to Sir Alexander Mackenzie. Mackenzie was an early fur trader and explorer, and he accomplished a magnificent feat when he led an expedition across Canada from Fort Chipewyan on Lake Athabasca to the Pacific Ocean. His incredible journey was completed in 1793, eleven years before Lewis and Clark began their famous expedition to the west. He's still remembered in Canada today for the feat. Mackenzie's earlier attempt in 1789, however, had been a major disappointment. His explorers had set out in an effort to find a water route to the Pacific. The valiant group followed a mighty river (now named the Mackenzie) with high hopes, paddling furiously amid great danger. Unfortunately, it didn't empty into the Pacific, but into the Arctic Ocean. In his diary, Mackenzie called it the "River of Disappointment."[27]

Unfortunately, we've all sailed on that river. Cleopas and his companion and a host of others have all spent time on the "River of Disappointment." What do we do when we find ourselves in those bitter waters?

The second part of the story answers that. When Cleopas and his companion finished telling this stranger what was going on, he commented on their news report, reminding them about what the Messiah would do and how he would suffer. When they finally arrived at the village, the two disciples urged him to stay with them. When they gathered at the table, their guest took bread, broke it and gave it to them. The words used here were almost identical to Jesus' words at the Last Supper. It was at that moment that the two disciples were finally able to really see. They understood who the stranger was. It was Jesus. Almost as soon as they knew, he vanished from them. Then they recalled that their hearts burned within them while he had been teaching them concerning the Messiah on the road to Emmaus.

What emerged from this unexpected encounter? The Lord is with us in our times of disappointment, not scolding us but with us encouraging us to see how he is at work. This is what Jesus did for Cleopas and his companion. He listened and then opened the scriptures to them to help them see that God was with them in the middle of what they were experiencing.

God hears and knows our frustrations as well. He walks with us during the hard times and encourages us. We don't just snap out of it, nor does the struggle just go away, but we can draw strength, comfort, and hope from the one who is present in life's most disappointing moments. I like what Max Lucado wrote, "He saw you cast into a river of life you didn't request. He saw you betrayed by those you love. He saw you with a body that gets sick and a heart that grows weak. He saw you in your own garden of gnarled trees and sleeping friends. He saw you staring into the pit of your own failures and the mouth of your own

---

[27] David Egner, "River of Disappointment," *Our Daily Bread* (July 1, 2001). https://odb.org/US/2001/07/01/river-of-disappointment

grave. He saw you in your own garden of Gethsemane and he didn't want you to be alone ... He would rather go to hell for you than to heaven without you."[28]

Sometimes our help comes from what's unexpected.

---

[28] Max Lucado, *Jesus: The God Who Knows Your Name* (Nashville, TN: Thomas Nelson, 2020), 138.

Fourth Sunday of Easter
John 10:1-10

Gateway

I lived in St. Louis for about a decade. St. Louis is known for quite a few things: Cardinals baseball. Italian restaurants. An unusual style of pizza. Perhaps, more than anything else, St. Louis is known as the gateway city to the west. The symbol of that is, of course, the Gateway Arch. The Arch reflects St. Louis' role in the westward expansion of the United States during the nineteenth century. The Arch is the world's tallest arch and is the official centerpiece of the Jefferson National Expansion Memorial, Gateway to the West Park. The park is a memorial to Thomas Jefferson's role in opening the West, to the pioneers who helped shape its history, and to Dred Scott who sued for his freedom in the Old Courthouse.[29] Historically, St. Louis was the city that became identified with western expansion. It was the gate through which many entered as Americans moved west toward the Pacific Ocean.

The gate is where you enter to get to where you need to go. Those of you that are fans of professional sports understand the significance of the gate. You can't just walk into a major league ballpark. You have to know the right gate in which to enter. You can't just walk into an NFL stadium where you want. You have to go through the gates.

Knowing where to enter a place is important. Have you ever been to a restaurant or a sports arena where you didn't know how to get in? It can be frustrating. Those who don't enter by the right door or gate are usually not reputable people. They're often called gatecrashers. Gatecrashing is bad in the entertainment world, and it is frowned upon, even illegal. Gatecrashing isn't

---

[29] Kimberlee Ried, "A Gateway to the West," *Prologue Magazine* 48, no. 3 (Fall 2016). National Archives https://www.archives.gov/publications/prologue/2016/fall/gateway-arch.html

cool in our culture, but it can be devastating when done with respect to the church. How, you ask? Jesus addresses it. Let's take a look.

As we continue on this Lenten journey, we come to a pastoral setting. We see a rugged, first-century sheep pen, a stone wall with a gate squarely in the middle. Most communities, in Jesus' day, would have a sheep pen like this. Several flocks of sheep would go in the sheep pen at night to keep them from wandering and getting lost. A watchman would position himself at the gate of the pen, literally becoming the gate himself. One could only go in or out through him. He was the gateway.

That's what we see about Jesus in this passage of scripture. John quoted Jesus about the importance of shepherds who care for the sheep and the wolves who do not. This is an image that would easily resonate with his listeners. In the first part of this text, Jesus talked about himself as the gate. That's what we'll pause to consider.

Gates are important and Jesus used the image of the gate in this text. Elisabeth Johnson wrote, "The function of the gate is to keep the sheep together in the sheepfold during the night, safe from thieves and predators. During the day the gate is opened so that the sheep can go out, following their shepherd, to find pasture. The gate and the shepherd work together for the well-being of the sheep, so that the flock thrives. Jesus is both the gate and the shepherd at the same time; he guards and protects his sheep from danger, and he provides for their nourishment, for their life in abundance."[30]

The image is one that his hearers would have readily known and with which they would identify. A sheep pen, gate, shepherds, thieves, robbers, and sheep. Jesus made a distinction between who comes in by the gate and who does not. Shepherds entered through the gate. Those who sought to harm the sheep, thieves and robbers, did not. Only those who come to the flock through the gate (Jesus) were legitimate. Those who came in by another way were intent on wreaking havoc and destruction.

---

30 Elisabeth Johnson, "Commentary on John 10:1-10," The Working Preacher (May 7, 2017). https://www.workingpreacher.org/commentaries/revised-common-lectionary/fourth-sunday-of-easter/commentary-on-john-101-10-3

We don't have to be in church very long to know that there are men and women, wolves in sheep's clothing, who are intent on destroying God's people rather than teaching, instructing, and nurturing. They may look like they belong, but they do not. They do not come in through Jesus and they don't care about the flock. The sheep don't know their voice and won't follow them. The wise church today follows the example of those sheep.

Jesus extended the metaphor of the gate in verse nine. "I am the gate. Whoever enters by me will be saved and will come in and go out and find pasture." He adds in verse ten, "I came that they may have life, and have it abundantly." Gifts await those who enter through Jesus.

He will come in and go out and find pasture. This is a powerful image that evokes a sense of freedom and fulfillment. Imagine the carefree life of a sheep that can come and go from the security of the pen to eat as much as he wants from lush, green fields. It's an abundant life. It is the kind of life that can be ours, if we'll enter through the gate.

A lot of times, in our culture, we seek fulfillment and meaning in the things of this world.

"If I can just get that promotion, then I'd be set."
"If I had that new car, my life would be so much better."
"All we need is a new, bigger house, then we'll be happy."
"I'd be happy if I had what she's got."
"Who doesn't need an 85-inch HD television?"

The truth is, though, these things never seem to completely satisfy. Why? Things don't ever bring satisfaction. They simply can't. Fulfillment isn't found in things. It's found in a person, Jesus Christ. He's the gateway that leads to abundant life.

There's more. Jesus noted that the one who enters through him will be "saved." There's a lot to be said for having fulfillment, security, and peace. As wonderful as those things are, they pale in comparison to the salvation found in Jesus. Max Lucado summarized the importance of salvation through Jesus in his book *Grace for the Moment*. He wrote, "Though the Bible was written over sixteen centuries by at least forty authors, it has one central theme — salvation through faith in Christ."[31] The gateway that leads to life and salvation. There's no better description of Jesus than that.

---

31 Max Lucado, *Grace for the Moment*, Thomas Nelson, Nashville, 2000, p. 266

Fifth Sunday of Easter
John 14:1-14

Homebuilder

There's something about home that strikes a chord with most of us. It doesn't really matter where we're from or where we've been, Dorothy's closing line in *The Wizard of Oz* resonates with poignant truth. "There's no place like home."

Folgers' Coffee capitalized on the yearning for home with their 1987 classic commercial "Peter Comes Home for Christmas." This commercial combined the best elements of Christmas into a clever coffee advertisement. Peter came home from college on Christmas Eve bearing gifts and was greeted by his excited younger brother. Together, the two brew a hot pot of coffee to wake up the rest of the family on Christmas morning. This ad continues to tug at the heart strings over thirty years later.

Home. It's more than a house or location. It goes deeper. It's shared life experiences with those you know and love. It's a place where we can be who we are without fear of rejection. The poet Maya Angelou understood the appeal of "home." She wrote, "The ache for home lives in all of us, the safe place where we can go as we are and not be questioned."[32]

As we're nearing the end of this Lenten journey, we turn our eyes toward home and our wonderful homebuilder, Jesus Christ.

The setting of this text is Jesus' farewell address at his last supper with his disciples. It is a time of uncertainty, confusion, and sadness. Jesus had washed their feet and had explained to them what it meant. He announced his betrayal by Judas who had slipped out into the night. He told his disciples that he would be with them only a little while longer, and that where he is going, they cannot come. Is it any surprise they were anxious?

Jesus responded to their anxiety by telling them, "Do not let your hearts be troubled. Believe in God, believe also in me."

---

[32] Maya Angelou, *All God's Children Need Traveling Shoes,* Random House, March 12, 1996, p. 196

He reassured them, "It's going to be all right." The tense of the Greek word for "believe," used twice here, implied "Keep on trusting me." Jesus was going back to his Father, which was incredibly good news for them. Then, he talked about home. There are many "dwelling places" in my Father's house. "And if I go and prepare a place for you, I will come again and will take you to myself, so that where I am, there you may be also."

Can you imagine how they felt hearing these words? The world, as they knew it, was falling apart. Nothing made sense. In the middle of troubling times, Jesus spoke about home. There are many dwelling places in his Father's house, and he goes to prepare a place for them. This is about more than just the "dwelling places." This is about being with Jesus and with God. It's about sharing in that close, personal relationship. I suppose, most simply put, it's about going home.

There are some important things to recognize about going home. First, you have to know the way. I'm always amazed at the stories we hear and read about dogs who've been separated from their owners who will go long distances just to get home. Every dog lover has heard a variation of the miraculous lost dog story. The pup who slipped her leash then made it home before her owners could get there. The dog who ran all the way home across town from the sitter's place. The rascal who disappeared into thin air, then showed up two weeks later with a stench, an appetite, and a wag of the tail. The 1993 movie *Homeward Bound* is loosely based on true stories of dogs that travel hundreds of miles to reunite with their owners. I am intrigued by how dogs are able to do that. How can they make such a long trip to reunite with owners?

They know the way back. Research suggests a couple of different ways dogs do it. One, of course, is by smell. The other is by using "compass runs" or sprinting north and south to establish their bearings. Then, according to the website "the dogs' incredible ability to find their way home seems to spring from an ability to detect magnetic fields."[33]

---

33 Mary Robins, "How Dogs Find Their Way Back Home," The American Kennel Club, https://www.akc.org/expert-advice/news/how-lost-dogs-find-their-way-home/, October 13, 2020.

I'm glad that's not how we find our way back home, aren't you? For us, the way home is simple and direct. We don't get there by doing enough good works. You can't stack enough good works together to build the bridge that leads to home. We don't get home by paying the fare. Money has nothing to do with our ability to go home. It's not based on connections or standing either. Who your father-in-law is and what he does for a living has nothing to do with you getting home. How do we get home? Jesus answers that. "I am the way, the truth, and the life. No one comes to the Father but by me." The road home leads through Jesus.

What makes home special? For some, it's the comfortable place you knew growing up. For others, it's familiarity. It's where you know everyone, and everyone knows you. For most people, home is special not because of how fancy it is, but because of who is there. That's especially true of the home Jesus promised. He told them, "You know me," so you know my Father, too. You've seen me, so you've seen my Father. Jesus was, I believe, speaking in relational terms here. The apostles had a close, personal relationship with him for nearly three years. They knew each other. Knowing Jesus is to know God. Even when Philip expressed some doubt, Jesus reassured him. "If you've seen me, you've seen the Father."

Imagine being in a place where there is perfect love. There are no secrets, guilt, or shame. All is known, forgiven, and released. The freedom that must accompany that has to be exhilarating. The sheer exuberant joy that must accompany living in such freedom has to be overwhelming. Truly, to quote Bart Millard, "I can only imagine."[34]

When I think of home, I don't really want a big, fancy house. I am not really interested in a swimming pool or garden side fountains. I'd rather have the home Jesus built for me and for all who come through him.

---

[34] Bart Millard (MercyMe), "I Can Only Imagine," The Worship Project (1999).

Sixth Sunday of Easter
John 14:15-21

Presence

It's hard to say "Good-bye." I've moved a few times while in the ministry, and it's never easy. It can be exciting to begin a new chapter and go to a different place, but the "good-byes" are tough. Even though we live in an age where video technology and smart phones have brought people together a whole lot more, hugs and smiles still mask the sad reality that it may be a long time before you actually see those you've loved again.

While "good-byes" are hard when people are simply moving, "good-byes" are exceptionally difficult when we're faced with the finality of death. Even for the Christian who knows where their loved one has gone, it can be painful to say that final, "See you later." As we approach the end of this Lenten journey, we are coming to the place where the disciples are told that Jesus is leaving. The scene takes place in the garden, just before the crucifixion. The brutality of what will happen in a matter of hours is pushed aside as Jesus tenderly spoke to his followers about what was to come. He was leaving this world, but he was not leaving them alone. The presence of Jesus in their lives and ours changes everything.

Jesus understood what saying "good-bye" was like. Just before his death, he addressed his leaving. He told them he was going away. How did they receive this? We don't know for sure. The text doesn't say.

When Jesus isn't there like we hope he'll be, it can leave us feeling lost, alone and empty. We feel as Martha did at the death of her brother. When Jesus finally came to Bethany four days after Lazarus died, she exclaimed, "Lord, if you'd been here, my brother would not have died" (John 11:32).

Where is Jesus when my mom and dad are fighting?

Where is Jesus when my marriage is falling apart?

Where is Jesus when my heart is reeling from the sting of rejection?

Where is Jesus when my children are struggling?

These are honest questions from hurting hearts. What is Jesus' response to this sad situation? "I will not leave you orphaned; I am coming to you. In a little while the world will no longer see me, but you will see me; because I live, you also will live" (vv. 18-19). He offers his followers an incredible promise, love, life, the Advocate, and his presence.

Five times in this short passage the word "love" is found. Love is demonstrated by keeping his commandments, and the thrust of the passage is clear. Those who love Jesus are loved by the Father. It is an inseparable bond. Trusting and being faithful, even in the most challenging times, makes us aware of his unfathomable love. When the dark clouds roll in and the booming thunder resounds, the words we learned a long time ago in Sunday school remain true and powerful. "Jesus loves me. This I know. For the Bible tells me so."

Jesus also told his disciples that, though he was going away, they would live. He said, "Because I live, you also will live." Jesus was speaking to his disciples before his crucifixion and his words had a sense of foreshadowing. The grave would not hold Jesus. Death would not have the last word. Real life begins when we are in Jesus and Jesus is in us. This may have been what Fanny Crosby wrote of as she penned words we all know well, "Blessed assurance. Jesus is mine. O what a foretaste of glory divine" (in the public domain).

Jesus promised to send them another advocate as well. The word in Greek here is the word transliterated "paraclete." It's a tough word to translate. It's been rendered "advocate," "counselor," "comforter" and "helper." In my view, all of them are good descriptions. The Holy Spirit is all of these things and so much more. When Jesus left the disciples physically, he promised that they would not be alone. The Holy Spirit would be with them. He's with us today, too. He directs, guides, nurtures, enables, and aids us in doing what God wants us to do. The Holy

Spirit is the person of God who dwells in believers today. As he led the disciples long ago, he'll do for us today.

When our Adversary whispers that you don't matter and no one cares about you, our Advocate rebukes him and reminds us of whose we are and who we are.

When our Adversary flings accusations against us, reminding us of what we used to be, our Advocate recalls how the price was paid for our sin. We are a new creation.

When our Adversary haughtily speaks of how we get what we deserve, our Advocate gently reminds of the amazing nature of grace.

The Holy Spirit, our Advocate, works with and for us, always.

The final part of what Jesus promised is himself. He will be with them. We've noted it once already in verse 18, but it's worth seeing again. Jesus said, "I am coming to you." He added in verse 20, "On that day you will know that I am in my Father, and you in me, and *I in you." (Italics mine.)* Jesus encouraged his disciples that even though he would not be with them in the physical realm, he would continue to be with them.

Jesus is present in our lives. Even when we can't see him, he's there. Even when we don't feel him, he feels what's happening to us. Even when we can't hear him, he hears our hearts and our cries. Jesus' presence in every part of our lives brings assurance, bolsters confidence, and inspires trust.

I heard the story of a little boy who was afraid of the dark. His mom tried everything from night lights to stuffed animals, but nothing seemed to alleviate his fear. One night, after putting him to bed and turning off the light, she sat by his bed and took his hand. He couldn't see her, and at first, he was frightened. "I'm right here," she reassured him. "I'm holding your hand." Even though the child couldn't see his mom, he was comforted by her presence as she held his hand. Before long he slept soundly.

Comforted by the presence; I like that. It works well for moms of little boys. It works well for followers of Jesus, too.

Ascension of the Lord
Luke 24:44-53

Ascended

M. Night Shyamalan is a well-known movie director. His movies include *Signs, Old, Glass,* and *Unbreakable.* My first experience with this creative director was with the movie *The Sixth Sense.* I will never forget watching that movie the first time and being totally astounded at the end. The ending put everything that went before it in a new light. I understood far better what had happened before because I knew the end.

In many ways, I think the disciples had that same feeling as Jesus, after the resurrection, began to teach and explain to them the scriptures and discuss all that had happened before. He "opened their minds" and then gave them a challenge that would change history and the world. Our Lenten journey is nearly over, but before we close, it's good to spend a moment or two with the ascended Jesus. The challenge he gave the disciples is still our challenge today.

Jesus challenged his followers then and now to be a witness of his life, death, resurrection, and the accompanying forgiveness of sins that is now possible. The word he used for "witness" is from the Greek word *martus*. This word means "one who testifies for or on behalf of." Jesus is challenging the disciples to share what they've seen, learned, and understood. Forgiveness of sins is to be proclaimed to all nations, beginning in Jerusalem.

Historically, we know the disciples met that challenge. They gathered in Jerusalem, and on the Day of Pentecost, the Holy Spirit descended on them. The church, as we know it, was born that day. Ken Curtis wrote, "The apostles were not the kind of group you might have expected Jesus to send forth on his mission to reach the world. There was nothing special or spectacular about them. The twelve apostles were just ordinary working men. But Jesus formed them into the backbone of the church and gave them the most extraordinary task imaginable: calling the entire world, including the mightiest empire ever known, to repentance and faith in the risen Christ. You can be sure that any educated, first-century Roman citizen would have laughed at any prediction that within three centuries the Christian faith would be the official faith of the empire."[35]

Jesus is still working through ordinary people today. You and I may not address emperors or kings as Paul did. We may not address foreign soldiers as Peter did. We may not meet leaders of other countries on the road as Philip did, but we are still called to be witnesses of what we've seen and what we know.

On this Lenten journey, we have had the opportunity to see Jesus remake the broken beautiful, offer hope to the hurting, see the invisible, embrace the lonely, and challenge the powerful. We've seen him pay the ultimate sacrifice and rise again, triumphant. There's a lot to which we can testify. The question is how. There are opportunities everyday for us to do that if we are looking for them.

It might seem like overkill to spend hours preparing a Sunday school lesson for just two kids, but it's an opportunity to bear witness to Jesus and what he means to you.

It could cost you an extra half hour of television time, but visiting your elderly neighbor across the street after work might just be a chance to share what you know about Jesus in both words and actions.

It's out of the way and it really ought to be his parents' responsibility to get him there, but going to get the boy who doesn't have a ride to church might be a way to witness to what Jesus means to you.

These are just the simple, everyday things we do, but they are real opportunities for witness if we understand and are aware of them. The next part is important. We can't do this by willing ourselves to do it. It won't happen just by our resolve. We will

---

[35] Ken Curtis, "What Ever Happened to the 12 Apostles?" Christianity.com, April 28, 2010, https://www.christianity.com/church/church-history/timeline/1-300/whatever-happened-to-the-twelve-apostles-11629558.html

become more aware of these chances and able to meet them if we rely on the Holy Spirit.

Jesus then reminded the disciples of the Holy Spirit, who would come upon them. The power to be the witnesses they needed to be would not happen through their own strength or ability. It would happen because the Holy Spirit would empower them. We know that's true. Zechariah 4:6 notes, "Not by might, nor by power, but by my spirit, says the Lord of hosts."
In the Disney classic, *Pinocchio*, we were introduced to Jiminy Cricket. He's a wonderful and memorable character. The famous line in his song to the puppet who would be a real boy is "Always let your conscience be your guide."[36] With all due respect to Jiminy Cricket, that advice ought to be amended just a bit. For followers of Jesus, the song should say, "Always let the Holy Spirit be your guide." When we follow the promptings of the Holy Spirit, we find ourselves where we need to be and doing what God wants us to do.

What happens after Jesus shares with the disciples about the Holy Spirit is nothing short of remarkable. There are two, possibly three, accounts of Jesus' ascension. While we don't know for sure why, I think the reason might be easy to understand. The "good news" was in the challenge. Jesus died and rose again. He conquered death and the grave. Forgiveness, life, and hope are offered through him. Bearing witness to that is a joy. Seeing Jesus leave, especially to those who spent three years with him in a personal way, had to be tough. That might not have brought them joy. However, for us two thousand years later, the ascension adds a wonderful glimpse into what's to come.

Jesus ascended to his Father. Luke simply wrote, "He withdrew from them and was carried up into heaven." It seems like such a simple, declarative statement, but its meaning and impact go far beyond those ten words. In those ten words we have the destination of this journey defined. The end of the road is not in church. The end of the journey is not ending the Lenten season. The end of the journey is spending forever with the Father. Jesus'

---

[36] Pinocchio, directed by Hamilton Luske (1940, Los Angeles, CA: RKO Pictures).

ascension reminds us of where we're going, where we're headed. It's been a wonderful journey. The ascended Jesus reiterates where we're headed at the end of the road.

Seventh Sunday of Easter
John 17:1-11

Glorified

Kansas City is my hometown. I've been a fan of Kansas City sports teams since my youth. The last few years have been exciting as a Kansas City sports fan. The Royals were in back-to-back World Series, winning in 2015. The Chiefs were in back-to-back Super Bowls, winning in 2020. Both of these were a bit unexpected and generated a parade and party in downtown Kansas City, the likes of which I had not seen before. Royals players Eric Hosmer, Salvador Perez, and Lorenzo Cain were honored. The Chiefs star players Patrick Mahomes and Travis Kelce also basked in the glory of winning.

There's something glorious about winning it all, accomplishing a great feat, or achieving something no one else ever has. As much as I enjoy sports and love the Kansas City teams, the glory they achieve is nothing compared to the glory we read about in John 17. In a prayer at the end of the Last Supper, before his crucifixion, Jesus spoke directly and honestly to his Father. He was praying about what he had done and what he was about to do. He prayed for his disciples and all who would come after them. It all centered around glory. We've come to the end of journey. It concluded with one last look at Jesus.

First, we want to see him in all his glory. "Glory," or a form of that word, is referenced six times in this passage. Jesus was anticipating finishing the work his Father called him to do. He would bring glory to the Father in doing that. As Craig Koester noted, "The word "glory" (Greek doxa) can have a fine sense of honor or brightness, yet the key to its role in John's gospel is that it has to do with the way God is made known to human beings."[37]

Jesus made the pathway to God known and, in doing so, revealed God to his lost people. Jesus' own glory then becomes the subject. He had glory from the beginning. John notes, that: "And the Word became flesh and lived among us, and we have seen his glory, the glory as of a father's only son, full of grace and truth" (John 1:14). That glory has been evident. Now, through the work he's about to do, it will be even greater. I don't think you can see Jesus without seeing his glory. Do you want evidence?

Look at the face of one who's just given his life to Jesus and listen to them talk. Can you sense the excitement and joy that emerges from them? Redeemed lives testify to the glory of Jesus.

Hear the testimony of one who was ensnared in a life of addictions and hopelessness. Catch how they describe their deliverance and what it means to them to at last be free. Restoration highlights the glory of Jesus.

Talk to a Christian who's facing a terminal illness. The confidence and assurance they possess that, despite what happens, God will be with them is a powerful witness. It emphasizes the glory of Jesus.

Spend time with one whose life is consumed with serving the Lord and others. What others might see as hard work, they view as joy and a blessing. Being poured out for the cause of Christ points to the glory of Jesus.

The glory of Jesus is all around us. Seeing it can encourage us in our own lives and motivate us to share his glory with others.

Our final look at Jesus is also one in which we see him pray for his disciples to be protected and to be one, even as he and the Father are one. The glory of Jesus is the radiant backdrop to this request. Because he will clear the way to the Father by atoning for sin, Jesus prays for his followers to be protected. This is a stark reminder that there are those who do not care about Jesus' glory and don't want to be confronted with it.

---

37 Craig Koester, Commentary on John 17:1-11, Working Preacher, June 5, 2011, https://www.workingpreacher.org/commentaries/revised-common-lectionary/seventh-sunday-of-easter/commentary-on-john-171-11

I love the 1989 movie *Glory*. It is a powerful movie about the 54th Massachusetts Volunteer Infantry from its organization in the winter of 1863 to the climactic assault of July 18, 1863, against Fort Wagner, a massive earthwork guarding the approach to Charleston. The 54th was led by Colonel Robert Gould Shaw and was the first all African American regiment in the Union Army. The theme of the historically accurate film is to see the 54th earn glory or respect despite those who didn't want to give it to them.

There are always those who refuse to respect and honor those they should. Jesus prayed for protection for his followers as they encountered those people.

The last thing he prayed for in this short passage was unity. The glory of Jesus is the unifying factor for believers. Who Jesus is and what he did combine to define his glory. His identity and work serve as the basis for our unity.

We may attend different churches, sing different songs, or read a different translation of the Bible, but if Jesus Christ is our Lord and Savior and our only way to heaven, we are brothers and sisters in Christ.

We may be of different races or backgrounds, have different expressions of worship or speak different languages, but if we agree Jesus is God's Son and have salvation through his death and resurrection, we are family.

I like the picture John painted in Revelation 7:9-10. He wrote, "After this I looked, and there was a great multitude that no one could count, from every nation, from all tribes, peoples, and languages, standing before the throne and before the Lamb, robed in white, with palm branches in their hands. They cried out in a loud voice, saying, "Salvation belongs to our God who is seated on the throne, and to the Lamb!"

What a glorious scene! What a glorious Savior!